Odes to Common Plants

Odes to Common Plants

By Dian Cunningham Parrotta

RESOURCE *Publications* · Eugene, Oregon

ODES TO COMMON PLANTS

Resource Publications
An Imprint of Wipf and Stock Publishers
199 W. 8th Ave., Suite 3
Eugene, OR 97401

www.wipfandstock.com

PAPERBACK ISBN: 978-1-7252-6063-4
HARDCOVER ISBN: 978-1-7252-6062-7
EBOOK ISBN: 978-1-7252-6064-1

Manufactured in the U.S.A.   01/13/20

Dedicated to my Aunt Mary Lou and my Aunt Gloria,

Who both always filled my childhood with multitudes
of flower gardens I still walk through today.

Contents

ode to plantain weeds | 1

ode to shamrocks | 2

ode to the wisteria trees riding roughshod over | 3

ode to foliar nyctinasty | 4

ode to that snowy feathery fringe trees | 5

ode to collecting the real flowers | 6

ode to the bloomed big leaf hydrangeas' puffy flower balls | 7

ode to Trader Joe's flowers | 8

ode to that *Sprig of Almond Branch in a Glass* | 9

ode to the dandelions and other edible wild greens | 10

ode to cactus ribs | 11

ode to the delicious lambs' quarters | 12

ode to pigweed | 13

ode to the garland | 14

ode to grassy lawns on hills | 15

ode to protruding dead branches on the backyard elm tree | 16

ode to crab grass | 17

ode to the ginkgo biloba tree and to her leaves | 18

ode to celebrating coastal sagebrush scrub | 19

ode to all the falling trees' leaves | 20

ode to the sap of the root stems of ferula asafetida | 21

ode to those pyrus calleryana or those callery pear trees
    and green crab apple trees | 22

ode to parsley | 23

ode to the delicious lambs' quarters | 25

ode to Balm of Gilead Tree | 26

ode to Boswellia Sacra—Frankincense Trees— | 27

ode to dillweed plant | 28

ode to the plantain weed

a Brobdingnagian broadleaf plantain
a circular universe

this round leafed plant
low circles of leaves,

low-growing pressed
close squatting real low

with flower stalks 12-18 inches tall
spike shells like firing silver bullets

cone-shaped bloom
bending its stem tight

arrowheads fly.
You are your own microcosmos

an intercontinental ballistic missile
control facility center

with medicinal properties with edible leaves and seeds
appreciated from far back.

Anglo-Saxons remedies for scrapes, wounds, burns, sores
bites and bee-bug stings.

A wide rosette spread
a common weed with wide, oval leaves

by Roman armies
on conquests.

You so remembered as *the white man's*
perennial footprint.

ode to shamrocks

deep green grass
with shamrocks
booming white
flowerets
three leaflets
closes tight
in the night
dreaming of
St. Patrick
with each leaf
Father, Son
Holy Ghost
faith, hope, love
oh young, sprig
Ireland's
character
glorious
the princely
diadem
like green glass

ode to the wisteria trees riding roughshod over

They, the Ports Professional Tree Surgeons, a local Pruning/Removal company, are scheduled to tackle—hack down my gangbustering wisteria tree monsters shimmering on stiffened tree trunk thighs hiding behind lovely drooping panicles of lilac and bluish-purple flowers and their sweet fragrances perfuming the front gardens from the front of my house but they won't be speaking to the heart of these wisteria wood won't till first of August. I told them they're tearing off the gutters, smothering the small Japanese oaks and the weeping willows and strangling the sleeping dogs. They're growing and entwining on the clematis planted on cedar trellis and the vines refusing to go down quietly. These climber creepers showing their bad sides. They want to cover everything. They are unwelcome and hostile takeovers. A Controlling mix of the mad Medusas and radioactive octopuses where unfortunate frogmen get attacked and no harpoon guns, daggers and no pruning shears can be enough to defeat terror of the deep clawing takeover. There is the good and the bad of wisteria with roots as vigorous as the top growth killing the foliage in their path. They're rampant vines with unstoppable insufferable blooms, like shiny lures on fishing lines, fragrant curtains of blossoms with trunks that twists, and curve and spin spun tangled warps and weft branches, their tapestries of flat woven into elegant design grabbers like sharply dressed treble hooks. And I will worry not a bit once it's night like the plants of nyctinasty like the blooming rose of Sharon, the gazanias, the green shamrocks, and sorrels all simply fold-up a petal foliar tucking themselves in for bedtime dreams.

ode to foliar nyctinasty

There are many examples of plants that include trees that display foliar nycti-
nasty, that closing leaves at night. The silver birches' branches and leaves sag like
in a charming and colorfully quaint tree siesta. Legumes have closing leaves,
beans, and peas close the tight only opening in the sunlight like closing clothes
shops in Salamanca from the medieval town of Avila to the beaches of Malaga.
The white daisy petals close at dusk too and follows the most embraced tradition
surrounding its yellow center till it's all just simply white. Gazanias too fold up in
low light and tulips tuck themselves in too. The blooming rose of Sharon is an-
other plant along with the shamrock, that low-growing clover with three lobbed
leaves too closes its doors at night both well known in the Bible and bless that
Trinity along with the wood sorrel and silk trees all have opening and closing
leaflets like in Spain they close up those shops that follow internal those com-
mon tradition clocks than the on-off environmental cues—- It's those circadian
rhythms of repeated patterns swing pulse to the beat of environmental iambic
like in poetry just like those living in an innate 'Spanishness' living in Madrid,
Spain and hear those tourists saying

"Oh, they closed down the kitchen."

ode to my father's favorite snowy feathery fringe trees

For the three days of the festival in Bethel, in Sullivan County, and on its southeast shore of Ulster landing Park in Saugerties where I was on vacation the same time Woodstock 1969 was held on a dairy farm in the Catskill Mountains, between Aug 15-19 and Jimi played on Monday at 9:00 a.m., the Star-Spangled Banner immortalized on film. There were lots of camping guests sleeping in Grandpa's creek and their floating white bars of ivory soap and nudity—in his waterfalls and I was watching them from the barn behind daddy's shooting target practice stakes and plates right by that brick fireplace. They had pitched up tents with campfires in the dark. Then early morning when my daddy wanted to go fishing for rainbow trout, chain pickerel, and bass, so we were pulling out the nightcrawlers and red wigglers from the worm pit, a big part of the slope, in his yard, behind and right past his shed and barn. We both saw them sitting where my I left my chalk sticks on my gray river flat creek rock and see pastel pink peace signs, yin, and yang, and some broken hearts and they released my bottled bubbles with my wand. And my daddy said they're smoking skunk on top of furred hawkweeds, the needlegrass, the prairie drop seed, and spike-like panicle foxtails curving upward wavy cylindrical and stones, and right under daddy's snowy feathery fringe'-trees with a big real blooming flocculent—a downy, my father's favorite shrubs of lilac-like smelling sweet. We traipse through daddy's secret places through those long shortcut ventures deep into grandpa's woods.

ode to the real flowers Karen was collecting

You collected tall green stem flowers with white laced tops. How nicely you could decorate their position within your two small hands and kicking Grandma Gee Bee's back side-door. Then standing backward, chubby, small dirty-faced and all. You spun around, extending your two arms out to a warm *"How beautiful."* And ran off to pick some more. I stayed behind and overheard that you were picking weeds all that time. Glanced at you there. There in the backwoods among the flowers. To me, they were *real flowers.*

ode to the bloomed big leaf hydrangeas' puffy pink flower balls

Sattaday morning and sitting on a first stoop step wishing it was shaded by leaves, but it's the closest to the ground where really important things are happening rather than somewhere else. There's a roly-poly pill bug, an armadillidiid, is crawling out from the more moistest of all spots and I'm wondering if it can float or not. He sees a leggy ladybug then stops. I aim a gust of air breath and curls inna ball.

"What do you wanna do?" Cornelius and his sister Winnann always hasta ask and show off their vocab-alary and how they can count by fives. I got on my brother's new pair of pink rubber-soled sea cadet shoes on all polished a bright so white and his sailor hat folded in a tight cloth boomerang. I did take them from his room.

The kids are coming out soon. I've already knocked on doors, but Kathy Keenan can't come out till noon and my brother is busy cracking heinie stick thermometers and pulling them apart and watching mercury spill out into a pouring silver puddle on the ground. Then Brenda, Podrick and Miles Furlong ask if we wanna make mud pie cakes behind their bloomed bigleaf hydrangeas' puffy pink flower balls where no adults can see and not even the bad kid who lives across the street, but only the hunkering birds and those black-capped chickadees celebrating their birds' nests in cavities can see us playing in the bushes till our curfew is the lightning bugs.

ode to Trader Joe's Flowers

In Memory of Aunt Mary Lou and Aunt Gloria

And now I too can afford some fresh flowers to put on my table at home where the woody scents and colors of the Ranunculus and Tulips all dressed in baby breath and greenery bring the relaxed atmosphere and mood of my day just like how it was as a young child seeing my Aunt Mary Lou and Aunt Gloria. Oh, how wonderful their smiles were right there like the soft sweet-smelling rose bouquets and bags of the five almond party favors always leftover from the Italian wedding parties. And if they showed up at my punch ballgame, I would hit-fist the pink Spalding ball high and far at least two sewers down the street bringing me superpower strength from these two sidewalk flowers in silent bloom found there flowering out of the concrete-pavement-cement standing there but now right here on my table with me bought from Trader Joe's are both of you are still right here with me in floral fragrance.

ode to that *sprig of almond branch in a glass*

I cracked open a seed shell from an almond tree and planted it in a regular old Mason jar glass and it's all now growing so gracefully in the make-shift flower-pot too small, reminding me of Vincent van Gogh's "Sprig of Almond Branch in a Glass," an oil on canvas blossoms with opening flowers. Van Gogh's work, a large series of paintings of flowering orchards: of almond, of pink peach, of flowering plum orchard, of small pear trees in bloom. Gogh's little still life studies of intricate natural designs awakening a serenity, a kind of hope in me. Look at those quinces, those lemons, those pears and grapes in shades of yellow, a little green, of blue, of red and of pink.

Painting optimism inside of me almost just as much as how my vintage jewel-toned, my National Wildlife Bird Scarf is to me. Resembling of gemstones but of birds that Black-Capped Chickadee, a Red Cardinal on a branch, a drab gray Wren with slate gray wings and back, and that Pygmy Nuthatch song-singing acrobatic there outta genuine silk, how it does to me with that breezy scenic view of wild birds see the cardinal, the blue jays sitting on white snowy branches: like a polyester still life, the artwork I always wear. And see how silly it plays the game of peek-a-boo with me as it only shows its white backside, the rump of the scarf on purpose to people, hiding the treasured snowbird scene from everyone but me as they all say, «Oh, how I love your pure white silk scarf you always wear. It›s nice against your snowy-white hair.» the birds only want me to see them and how they all flutter-shakes themselves, switching their single stand-up leg with the other, it's a back and forth, trying to keep themselves warm. I see that little-tree-sparrow bird in the lower far right corner, fluffing its feathers to trap the heat, looking like a blow-up-feathered-puff-fish ball, there among the snow-filled branches because as soon as I am alone, the scarf, it becomes an alive digital motion-moving mural, a mesmerizing beauty, an almost certain cabalistic sign, so esoteric, so impenetrable, its magical realism happening. is alive like when you visit Café Terrace at Night. it's so secretive and so cliquish, in Arles, the south of France, where Ghost van

Gogh sets up his easels and his paints and his drying oils and you see him there painting sharp contrasts between the warm yellow, greens, and orange colors and the deep blue starry sky. the deepest paint of Prussian blue, cadmium yellow and chrome mixed with his brush stroking. that vibration of him doubling his gladness and pleasures into the illumination and contrast of the orange café floor, the egg-shaped tabletops, the window and the doors with those disseminated disks of stars so high there in his nighttime sky, painted without black, but in beauteous blues and violets and sage and citron greens.

ode to the dandelions and other edible wild greens

Just the thought of you made my Grandpa Mike make me kidnap him for a two-hour respite from the old age home without checking him out with no permission was worth those angry nurses. We were meandering out for a saunter through down the street and walked the block to his home. Grandpa Mike with a laryngectomy talked out of that throat hole and had the handshaking Parkinson's was a barrel of a man looking like a short Leonardo da Vinci with the nose. Once we got into his house (his house key silently hiding inside a weed). He turned on a Turner film and said *let's do Sunday supper* and went out the back door to harvest the weeds. The wild dandelions with the whorls of loose branching clusters of sheep sorrel with its long arrow-head ark green blades of bliss the lambs quarters clover chickweed and mallow weeds with its tender tips and shoots and leaves and roots he washed soaked boiled fried them with garlic onion red pepper flakes the olive oil and I salted boiling water and in the spaghetti until al dente but forgot the Sunday tomato sauce and we had no Parmigiana-Reggiano

ode to cactus ribs

So, you never fell in love did you Mr. Israeli man? Sleeping so soundly as I kiss your cheek a goodnight kiss goodnight. Walking across the parquet parlor floors to the exit door barefoot holding my walking shoes in hands clutched I leave you tucked in tightly shutting a door lightly behind me stepping down those stairs alone, quietly. Will I return tomorrow for another goodnight kiss to soothe my mighty needs and aches to brush across your bloomed desire growing out of its thorn rib cage where it knows not of seasons as of summer or of spring but lives as endless day of bloom an endless day in vast breath and pulse. I don't pick flowers Mr. Israeli man though smelling them comes easy the pleasure is all too sweet. my cactus ribs are curious and thorny protects my woody stems my flowers are large and colorfully hot hallucinogenic and thirsty where green lace roses daisies never stem into a grace.

ode to the delicious lambs' quarters

You, an annual wild edible, produce seventy-five thousand seeds used to be used by American Blackfoot Nation during the sixteenth century.

Oh, dusty-looking plant with a white coating on its leaves where rain-water beads run off your goosefoot shapes. You are a common weed always angrily picked and torn and thrown right out ever knowing you, ever knowing you are edible and nutritious. But now some winter-blanch and freeze your leaves like how I learned to do with that pigweed. Oh, how tasty your lambs' quarters hummus, quarter dock crackers, sesame seeds and wilted green sauté, and salt and vinegar lambs' quarters and chicken weed wrap, and garlic mustard stuffed mushrooms and lambs' quarter spread and lambs' quarters gnudi so steal the show at potlucks when you add the colorful ingredients of broccoli sprigs and grapes and tender farfalle pasta with golden beets, green and pine nuts.

ode to pigweed

pigweed or Amaranthus better said
a bushy shubby
tall in uninvited places with thousands

of dense inflorescences flower clusters small
and greenish with set shiny dark
reddish-brown to black seeds tiny

where gardeners love to hate
but some lovingly cultivate its leaves
to make a nice tasting tea or use its

seed to be sprouted and easy to harvest
and very nutritious with medicinal
values and a rich ornamental

plant almost like a lovely song like
Speak Softly, Love, that theme song.
A summer annual weed

who has a dramatic history? a forgotten food
think ancient civilizations like the Aztecs
with their feather-work with their

poetry prayers to the sun
and poems about fishing to music with flutes,
shells, and whistles and drums.

They played music
for the gods for the harvest
to be good they prayed for the growth of the Amaranthus tall

as male statues sitting
with their knees up and their arms
crossed and females' hands on their knee stone sculptures.

ode to the garland

A festoon of flowers
a garland of laurel
an aromatic evergreen
with dark green glossy leaves.
The eucalyptus of seven hundred species of flowering trees
bring meaning for the seasons.
It's a circular shaped journey of growth and everlasting life.
Garlands of flowers on Egyptian mummies
in celebration in entering the afterlife.
A part of religious ritual and tradition
from leaves, flowers, and branches festive occasions on holy days'
rituals with the changing seasons and fertility.
A beacon of creativity
hanging on one's front door seasonal or timeless circles of garland
cycles of the seasons so symbolic of our luminaries
the sun and the moon
garlanded silver and seeded.

ode to grassy lawns on hills

Rolling down grassy hills to the next
life's pilgrimage leaving
the clover standing.
Smell the freshly cut grasses
of late Saturday afternoons
on long Island
where the Jupiter bushes hold blue cut glasses
like lost rings glimmering, vibrantly jewel'd

ecstasies of children whorls and spirals
all the laughs and giggles
that sweet vertigo's
sizzy senses of motions
of skies and grasses switching locations
and back again spinning
the grassy public parks make perfect spots for a wedding
ceremonies and receptions.
Historical plantations with formal gardens
and rocky slopes forested with unusual soil and rocks,

rare plants on green grassy hills.
Oh, the burning bushes,
fragrant sumac
and Japanese yews
the growing
creeping junipers
or liriope, grass-like, flowering plants on slopes
falling suddenly into standing sprays & wreaths among
    the white daffodils
down which we roll our one last-movement like a classical
    style orchestral piece.

ode to both the protruding dead branches
on the backyard elm tree

Ekphrasis Poem Tribute to Giselle (Royal Opera Ballet)
sculptures of fine art beauty in three dimensions
cast metal and unfired clay arms outstretching over young shoulders
and a ballerina's strong dancer's legs midair muscles in balance
overhanging tree branches in the dark
Giselle a masterwork
a peasant girl who dies of a broken heart
sylph-like movements of the lower branch
elegant posture and graceful
arms thereof a ballerina
swan arms forward folding

flying
down with spacing fingers spread wide
and here in my gazebo in the dark
seating is everything
chorister seat gives me a bird's eye view
a quintessential tale of heartbreaking loss and triumphant forgiveness
free no tickets required
then bamboo's younger shoots in two rows of twenty corps de ballet
dressed in wedding gowns like swans in a lake

fly an up and bens lower and lower like with the weight of snow
mirror the night-time stars mystical magic in moonlit wood
I stand up in and with my two applauding hands
then the neighbor's back porch lights go bright
making swans into bamboo trees then
back into swans again when their porch light shuts off
a chiseled headstand balances on elbows
the elm tree's dead branches like a metal sculpture abstract

ode to crabgrass

Crabgrass, may I go fishing in your carp mouthed lawn with bitters of man-like teeth? I'll wear my fashionable and functional wallaroo hat and my waterproof fly-fishing gloves. And look there goes big beetle May bug, that buzzy cockchafer, doodlebug passing by, such a cute clumsy fellow thinking about feeding on the leaves and flowers. Emerald green crabgrass bulbs you are a look of awe. You grass carps of coarse thick bladed circular patches on a fly. You are tight circles of aggressive blue crabs rising claws toward enemies while scuttling in clumps on the edges cheerfully always sideways in the wind just like fiddler crabs and those banana drumming claws scrambling sprawls and spreads out some purple color or bluish-grey intermingling with the crabgrass with the tall seed stalks with larger blades and thicker stems always spreading out evenly making angular turns showing off their crab leg clusters on top some ragged beds of pudding-stones some brown and deep red encircled off by sandy or cement as though it all is on a swiftly flowing stream or a beach with strong waves encircling by but here on my front lawn where carpets of moss, ivy, and weeds of crabgrass donning costumes of creatures of the sea.

ode to the ginkgo Biloba tree and her leaves

Now it comes to me that you fan-shaped leaves right in front of the Keenan's house, in Brooklyn on New York Avenue two duplex doors down from my old house cause we had a parking sign pole instead of a tree and there were those leaves now I know was from a Gingko Biloba tree—fell yellow. I didn't know your name then or why your golden fall lobed leaves, like tiny Japanese paper fans, fell differently than the Giordano's maple tree. Now feeling the fresh fall air just reminiscing about you. You are not like the maple, the sycamore, or the sweetgum tree. Thinking of always seeing you in yellow fall on the avenue with your parted cleavage scattering in sheer fall camisoles with one missed blouse button and though you are classy, you are from a street tree, a living fossil 350 million years old making you the oldest tree on earth from the era of dinosaurs. You are the earliest of my leaf-time memories of not thinking you were really a leaf. You Ms.—silver apricot—maidenhair tree, every leaf brings me right back to you.

ode to celebrating coastal sagebrush scrub

A weathered fence along the coastal soft chaparral's silvery carpet, fifty shades gray blur a weather-beaten fence lined with cowboy boots slipped over tops of posts on roadsides of all shapes and sizes down a rolling farm field's and shorelines with metal of lash and scourge, strung up barbed-wire from post to post on the old hickory stakes——That majestic tree stump trunk like a marine mammal like a Moby Dick that great Basin Bristle cone pine not far from an iconic windmill there with wooden slatted fan wheel and a rudder-like a tail has a quaint decorative feel of that silhouette of the American West. It's early a.m. in the dark or in the very first dimmest light a foxy brown thrasher with a long curving bill that rusty red songbird singing from the sage bush shrub with observing yellow eyes calling a series of repeated bits and trills celebrating the sage bush branches in a tangled mass of shrubbery with shriveled, darkened stems. A deer skull sits in snow. There's a black-billed magpie, swaggering a strut to the spicy bitter smells of the frosty bitten hedge line, caroling an ascending call and with a raspy chatter, short and a repetitive twice, thanking the soft chaparral, the low scrubland plant wock wock wock wock wock wock so sounding like a barking small dog and seagulls' shrills. And far left there is breakfast for one lone browsing pronghorn antelope feasting on a ready source of winter nutrition of woody stems and shrubs of sagebrush in snow.

ode to the falling trees' leaves

"The only constant is change," *(Heraclitus)* but isn't there a beauty in
the letting go various shades of two by two colors like yellow-orange or
like when you cut open orbital ovals into three equal wedge crescents
or citrus wheels and there are those slivered slices of the warm colors
of sun or fire then there are the cool colors calm soothing recede
making those spaces seem larger think calming blue waters through
violets and grays greens. those falling leaves in a brilliant show from
red, yellow to orange to bronze to browns of dried herbs of peppermint
leaves, lavender, chamomile, borage, caraway and catnip from sunlight
to cool nights of fallen that falling down autumn's phase of ripeness
before winter's old age dies like in a dripping candle clock or in
Western Europe's in Prague's times striking inside of that Astronomical
Clock with an allegorical parade of animated sculpture rings on the
hour every day. look at autumn's equinox and the pair of balance scales
of Libra represented by an inanimate, that sign of justice, balance, and
harmony of the creeping barrage in our gigantic space of earth—our
ephemeral universe but bringing the unchanging that fifth element, the
only constant that does not change that stereotype of our epitome of
a calm a perpetual and eternal unvarying. keep and hold on tightly to
the quintessence of your calm and never letting it go

ode to the sap of the root stems of asafetida

Agra and Delhi would eat a spoonful of the sap of your root stem with butter and practice on the banks of the river Yamuna enhancing their singers' voices. You, the sap of the roots and stems of the asafetida, the important perennial herb growing from classical antiquity unpleasantly strong a "devil's dung" while raw, is that they say that "stinking gum" but reminiscent of leeks, onions and garlicky, radiating flavor with an unforgettable aroma. You transform meals from a hint of you inside of the savory. Alexander the Great carried you, like a mysterious, an expensive prize, Ms. Stick Finger, he took you west in 4 BC. You are that decisive presence in Indian cooking. You are a pungent bouquet, my scarlet rose. The one most crucial ingredient in vegetarian cuisine from species of giant fennel, Ms. Asafoetida Hing, you carry the powder unique smell flavors, simply strong raw, a mellow garlicky. I stand up for you and I applaud you, my Ms. historically important herb, straight from classical antiquity from the deserts of Iran and mountains of Afghanistan, a superstar, cultivated in nearby Pakistan and India. You are the stellar aery that ethereal spice that extension of all a yearly springtime, that evanescence of all those gossamer things. You, that aromatic shocker to the western palette who keep you tightly stored in rubberized seal on the rim in plastics, in those airtight clip clamp lid containers—and in small airtight jars.

ode to those pyrus calleryana or those callery pear trees and green crab apple trees

see my older brother Kenny and me walk down those alleyways barefooted on Brooklyn, New York's Parkville Avenue, to Judy's house to sit on her swing; we are four and five years old. we turn right down a hot city cemented side alleyway, like a buried secret lane where Coney Island Avenue in those borderlands where Kensington meets Ditmas Park meets Parkville, running behind shambling, double porched homes. hold your breath like when you are going through the Brooklyn Battery Tunnel in the family's station wagon cause those pyrus callery-ana or callery pear trees and green crab apple trees smelling like a big stink up of rotting fish or of nanna's nasty feet-slipper smell, and the weeping cherry trees dangling, and drooping branches of glossy, dark green leaves with their blossoms atop like fallen white snow fountains captivating fragrances. each tree acting out like old men concierge of sorts in a phony- faux-class bouncer- police officers who lead the way to the hidden elbowmold smelling decrepit old-peoples' mildew-musty houses back there, and they're on our right, is Judy's swing painted pink I go right into her backyard pretending to be carrying roasting sticks I carry on camping trips but are carrying broken branches with dog doodie on the tips, just looking like grub sticks like burnt-barbecued marshmallows on a homemade-skewer kit . . . and stinking up like dead stink-stank-stunk-skunks' stench and I wipe-*touch* that poop on her swing good. and yell out, "Judy, Judy gots doggie doodie on her swing" run laughing-away, me pretending to be pigeon-toed on purpose and in a giggling-like stomach aching fit grab some cool-to-the-touch crabgrass bulbs inside of my toe-fingers and in fast motions in some somer-saults, handstands, cart wheelings thinking we are getting so far away. laughing, laughing, laughing, spinning around and around like our plastic push and the spin carousel spins. the sun moves up and down from the sky switching places with me and with the *the* old man concierge on one stiffened thigh like a twirling baton in the sky **hear** Judy's mom catapults out like a short stouted thunderbolt outta the back screen door, go-BANGBOP as that lady's arms akimbo and her eyebrow going up up and she fliPfloPsflipsfloPsfliPs flopping, flies me up like fake vomit hitting blue sky with a dirt-a-turd-crap-and-poo-ME up while my brother loping down the paved alleyway feet dip dip dip slaps smacking the hot cement, running longer and longer away like an avalanche

ode to Italian parsley

Italian parsley!
  Hey, flat leaf. How ya doing?
  Hey, man, I'm talking to you.
You're a powerful Italian American
possibly crime family related Colombo? Bonanno?
Aww no, the Gambino from New York City?
Family's from Naples, Italy like my Great Grandma Mary Trotta.
She's got your name. They used to call her daughter, my grandma, Tessy,
parsley
like you
forgetaboutit

she
was
in
everything.
Amen.

All over the place kinda gal.
At least that is what she told me
but I promised not to tell
she said, *don't tell nobody my nickname.*
She was flat too. No relations to curly

not at all. I mean she was not into the fancy
not into the garnish
or the decorative kind of thing.
She was into more of the robust
that flavorful cooking than most.

Flat, I like your outfit. It suits you.
You got your ruffled sleeves
Your Italian cut
A nice dark flat green
shinier than most I've seen.

Ralph Lauren? Alfani? Oh, Carlo Pignatelli. Nice. Real nice.
Love the dark green satin matching shirt and tie
Like that flashy a confidence builder
I mean you must know how that goes. We're old-timers now and
You know nobody cares about old people.
We're practically invisible, but hey, you're seen everywhere
You're in everything. God Bless.

ode to the delicious lambs' quarters

You an annual wild edible
you produce 75,000 seeds
used to be used by American Blackfoot Nation
during the sixteenth century
Oh dusty looking plant with a white coating on its leaves
rainwater beads run off
of your goosefoot shaped leaves
a common weed always angrily picked and tore and threw right out
never knowing you
knowing you were edible and nutritious
throughout winter blanch and freeze your leaves like how I do
    with the pigweed
oh how tasty your lambs quarters hummus,
quarter dock crackers, sesame seeds, and wilted green sauté, salt and
    vinegar lambs' quarters and chicken weed wrap,
garlic mustard stuffed mushrooms, lambs' quarter spread and gnudi

ode to balm of Gilead Tree

Your smell is a strong pleasant perfume with will be sticky and resinous a balsamic and fragrant buds, resinous and strong-smelling turns fingers reddish-brown with gum. The balm of Gilead is first mentioned in the Bible, *Gilead was a mountainous region east of the Jordon River Divided among the tribes of Reuben, Gad, and Manasseh* (Genesis 31:47-48). Sung in traditional African American spiritual song: *There is a Balm in Gilead/To make the wounded whole;/There is a balm in Gilead/To heal the sin-sick soul (en.m.wikipedia.org).* Poe mentions it in his "The Raven" *Respite—respite and nepenthe, from thy memories of Lenore;/ Quaff, oh quaff this kind nepenthe and forget this lost Lenore!"/*

Homer's Odyssey *"Nepenthe pharmakon" first appears the one that chases away sorrow that banishes grief from a person's mind and replaces it with blissful ignorance . . . so drinking to quaff a potion will soothe the pain of loss; this drug of forgetfulness.* A fragrant medicinal resin, the Gilead Tree is forgotten like now a "trash" tree on roadsides, in ditches. Bordering swamps those wet areas on the outskirts, now so forgotten like old broken armchairs tossed out far in the peripheries in the dumps.

ode to boswellia sacra—frankincense trees—

Here comes the holiest of the Christmas season
the one of the three gifts that the Magi bestowed
on the infant Jesus
the frankincense tree
like lifting a veil of the oldest of fragrances of bakhoor incense.
Frankincense plays a major role in Arabia since the dawn of civilization
that large tree that grows in dry mountainous
dusty places—the shrub's gum
a raggedy Boswellia sacra,
the frankincense tree still dances
so deserving to dress up in a beard
a Queen Hatshepsut's dressed as a man
she deserved to be pharaoh
like god Horus
in tree form
like a king in traditional robes
so deserving
in her own right

ode to dillweed plant

My anthium graveolens, my dillweed plant,
so aromatic green
standing on a sheathing foot
a cylindrical thin hollow
stem stalk
clan with shiny, delicate blue-green filiform
tangy flavor and a fragrance with finely divided feathery leaves
flat umbels with yellow flowers and small rolled-inward petals
pungent and bitter dilly
from the middle ages used by magicians
in their spells and charms
attracting love and abundance
protection from the jealous. I praise your magical powers said in all plant lore, legends and inside poets' lyrics that you are the protection against blasphemies protection against profanities and bad dreams. Your stalks along with a stick of dogwood put in the cradles protecting the newborns and always considered sacred to the Egyptian god Horus.

You waken the sacral chakra awakening our feelings and sensations. Oh, what the Persian lima bean basmati rice does to me more than its crispy golden tahdig crusty with saffron threads but with you, Anethum, with you, you a multitude of feathery thin green wisps flavorful and fragrant so mouthwatering.

www.ingramcontent.com/pod-product-compliance
Lightning Source LLC
Chambersburg PA
CBHW071801020426
42331CB00008B/2361